KARATE
Made Easy

Ralph Corrigan
Illustrated by Deborah Dutko

Sterling Publishing Co., Inc. New York

To my very special niece Lily Van Dyk,
whose early interest in learning karate inspired this book

I am indebted to many people who have helped me to appreciate the way of the martial arts. My deepest gratitude goes to Sensei Sid Gottlieb, whose knowledge and expertise in karate never cease to amaze me, who over the years has served as a model of teaching excellence, and who graciously agreed to read an earlier version of this book.

Next, I thank my son, Ralph III, for his advice on the wording of several passages, and his willingness to share his extensive martial arts knowledge with his dad.

Special thanks go to Donna Newlan, Robert Sicignano, Ivan Potje, Tom Whitmore, Yuko Konishi, Ilda and Joao Velez, and John Berrios for serving as models for several illustrations in this book.

Finally, I wish to thank Claire Bazinet for her expert editorial advice.

Book design and illustrations by Deborah Dutko
Edited by Claire Bazinet

Library of Congress Cataloging-in-Publication Data
Corrigan, Ralph
  Karate made easy / by Ralph Corrigan ; Illustrated by Deborah Dutko
    p.   cm.
    Includes index.
    Summary: Introduces karate for young people including upper and lower body techniques
    to learn (punches and kicks) and tracking sequences to practice.
    ISBN 0-8069-1370-3
      1. Karate for children -- Juvenile literature.   [1.Karate.]
  I. Dutko, Deborah, ill. II. Title.
  GV1114.32.C67 1995   95-21954
  796.815 -- dc20   CIP
                                            AC

10 9 8 7 6 5 4 3 2 1

First paperback edition published in 1996 by
Sterling Publishing Company, Inc.
387 Park Avenue South, New York, N.Y. 10016
© 1995 by Ralph Corrigan and Deborah Dutko
Distributed in Canada by Sterling Publishing
c/o Canadian Manda Group, One Atlantic Avenue, Suite 105
Toronto, Ontario, Canada M6K 3E7
Distributed in Great Britain and Europe by Cassell PLC
Wellington House, 125 Strand, London WC2R 0BB, England
Distributed in Australia by Capricorn Link (Australia) Pty Ltd.
P.O. Box 6651, Baulkham Hills, Business Centre, NSW 2153, Australia
Manufactured in the United States of America

Sterling ISBN 0-8069-1370-3 Trade
            0-8069-1371-1 Paper

Contents

Getting Started

This book offers a simple, step-by-step introduction to the art of karate. Easy-to-follow, self-teaching lessons, illustrated with drawings, show you exactly how to perform the basic karate punches and kicks. By the time you learn all the exercises and techniques taught in this book, you will have acquired a sound foundation in karate training.

Karate is an ancient martial art. The word itself is really two words: "kara" and "te," which mean "empty hand." Because weapons were outlawed, practitioners of karate — often called "the weaponless warriors" — created a system of self-defense that turned the human body into a formidable weapon. Through rigorous training methods, karate students toughened and strengthened the hands, fists, elbows, knees, and even the head, fashioning all these parts of the body into weapons to block attacks and strike an opponent.

But karate is really much more than punches and kicks. First, it is the best of all exercise programs, giving you an incredible all-around workout. It can be practiced year-round in the privacy of your own home, and karate knows no age limits. This book is written especially for young people, but whether you are five or seventy-five years old you can still benefit from the study of karate.

Secondly, karate is a total mind–body program. It keeps the mind mentally alert and focused, and it stretches and strengthens the body. Centering the mind on the task at hand, ignoring all distractions, is a crucial part of karate training. Likewise, the yoga-like stretches and the repetition of punches and kicks build a well-coordinated, supple, muscular body — ready for action!

Most importantly, karate helps you to overcome your fears by building self-confidence. If you sometimes feel insecure or even intimidated by others, by keeping up your karate training you will discover those insecure feelings fading away. Karate training makes you feel good about yourself. It promotes excellent mental health, and develops self-confidence because you know you can defend yourself if necessary.

All you really need to begin the study of karate is contained in this book. Each chapter starts with a brief discussion of an important karate concept, then introduces new upper- and lower-body techniques, and finally explains how the punches and kicks work in fighting situations. But to get the most out of this book, you first need to think about how to set up a sensible training program.

Developing a Plan

Before beginning, you need to develop a plan for your study of karate. To do this, think about the answers to these questions:

- How often should I practice?
- How much time should I devote to each session?
- How should the training sessions be set up?
- How long should I work on each lesson?
- Where should I practice?
- Who should I practice with?

Here are some suggestions:

HOW OFTEN SHOULD I PRACTICE? Young people often fall in love with karate and want to practice all the time. Unfortunately, some want to become instant black belts, and so they train extra hard for a month or so, then become confused and frustrated when they fail to reach their goals. The lesson here is to set realistic goals.

Karate training can't be rushed, so start slowly. Don't place too much pressure on yourself. Think of where you want to be in your training a year from now, or in five years!

Most of all, be consistent. Set aside certain times each week for practice, and keep to your schedule. Don't rush ahead on the lessons or you could find yourself losing interest or getting burned out.

If possible, start with three workouts a week. A Monday – Wednesday – Friday schedule makes a lot of sense. Your body can relax between sessions, and the weekends will be free. Two workouts a week are okay, but three will produce the best results. As you become more advanced, you can add more time to your workout schedule.

In fact, karate can be practiced whenever you have a few moments to spare. For example, while waiting for a school bus in the morning you could be going over the karate techniques in your mind, picturing yourself performing the moves correctly. This is called "imaging," and it has proven to be a valuable training exercise. Or you could be watching a TV show and doing your stretches at the same time. So even though you set aside formal workout times during the week to train, you can "practice" karate anytime and anywhere.

HOW MUCH TIME SHOULD I DEVOTE TO EACH SESSION? The time spent learning and practicing karate depends on you. In the beginning, you'll need at least fifteen minutes for warm-ups (stretching and conditioning exercises), then about a half hour to work on the techniques in each lesson. As you work your way through the book, repeating the exercises then adding new techniques, you'll discover each workout taking an hour or more.

HOW SHOULD THE TRAINING SESSIONS BE SET UP? Setting up your training sessions is easy. Just follow this simple structure:

- **Formal Bow** This traditional bow is performed at the beginning and end of every workout. See page 16 for specifics on the bow.

- **Warm-Ups** These are stretching and aerobic exercises that ready your body to perform the karate exercises. All the warm-up exercises are explained in the following chapter.

- **Basics** Next, practice the basic punches and kicks you have already learned. Perform each upper-body technique ten times on each side, then work through the lower-body basics.

- **New Techniques** Each lesson includes one new upper- and lower-body technique. After you have practiced the basics you know, then work on learning the two new techniques.

• **Tracking** Tracking exercises show you how to move back and forth while throwing punches and kicks at imaginary opponents. After finishing the basics, practice the tracking exercises you have learned in the previous lessons, then go on to the new tracking exercise.

• **Kata** Finally, after you have learned the lessons through to the last chapter, you will begin the study of *kata* (KAH-TAH) and add it to your practice. Kata is a performance of karate techniques, complete with drama and timing. It consists of sets of blocks, punches, and kicks thrown at several imaginary attackers. Kata comes last in the book because you need to learn all the techniques perfectly first. In the kata, you work to integrate the punches and kicks into dramatic sequences. In a regular workout, kata practice follows the basics and tracking exercises.

If you are curious about some of the advanced lessons (to see what is in store for you), by all means take a look. But remember that each lesson in this book builds on the previous one. So for the best results, you need to start at the beginning and study one lesson at a time.

HOW LONG SHOULD I WORK ON EACH LESSON? If you follow the three-workout-a-week schedule, you should be able to move through a lesson in one week. In the first session of the week, after the warm-ups and the repetitions of all the techniques learned so far, perform the two techniques in the new lesson slowly, concentrating on the proper form. Next, work on the new tracking exercise.

In the second session of the week, after repeating the basics and tracking exercises, review the instructions on both new techniques, then practice throwing the punch and kick, over and over. Finish the session with a review of the new tracking exercises in the lesson.

By the third session of the week, you should be able to perform the new techniques covered in the lesson with only a glance at the instructions. Now you can concentrate on adding more speed to the punches and kicks.

Since each workout repeats all the techniques already learned, you are constantly refining the moves while getting a strong aerobic workout. Repetition, if you haven't guessed it already, is the key to success in karate. The repetitions train your body to throw devastating punches and kicks.

WHERE SHOULD I PRACTICE? Here's where you can have some fun. You can create a place to work out — called a **dojo** (DOH-JO) — right in your own apartment or home. Your room, a playroom, or some space in the attic or cellar will work just fine.

Once you decide where to practice, think about decorating the space with your favorite karate pictures and posters. Be creative. Select materials that remind you of the importance and seriousness of karate training.

WHO SHOULD I PRACTICE WITH? This book is organized in self-teaching lessons, so you really don't need anybody to help you practice. But sometimes it is more fun to share a new interest with a good friend, or a brother or sister, or even with your mom or dad.

But remember: if you train with someone else, never throw a karate punch or a kick at the other person. Sparring of any kind is not

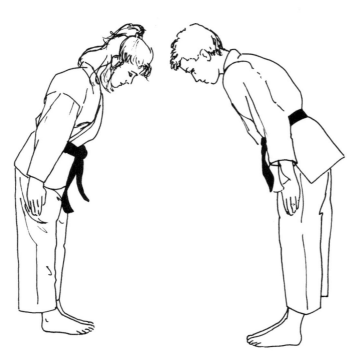

allowed unless a qualified black belt instructor is present. That means you can practice together, but you can't use one another as targets. Of course, if you are attacked on the street, then you can use your karate techniques with as much force as necessary to stop the attacker from hurting you.

The Teachings of the "One Heart Way"

The style in this book is based on a popular Okinawan karate system called **Isshinryu** (ISH-IN-ROO), which is world-famous for its straightforward, no-nonsense approach and its balanced emphasis on upper- and lower-body techniques. "Isshin" means "one heart" and "ryu" means "way" or "school," so Isshinryu karate is known as the "one heart way."

Masters of the "one heart way" teach that it is most important for the karate student, called a **karateka** (KAH-RAH-TEH-KAH), to develop a "good heart."

- First, students work to develop an attitude of respect towards themselves and others. This is the students' most important goal.

- Second, true karatekas never boast about karate, and are never bullies or show-offs.

- Third, the students listen to the wisdom of the karate masters, who teach that other parts of life are important too — like honoring parents, meeting all responsibilities to family, showing respect to teachers in school, and receiving good grades.

Karate training is often thought of as walking along a path that leads to perfection. Many people are travelling on this path. Some take two steps forward and one step backwards, others fall off the path completely, while still others move briskly ahead. Only you can decide how fast and how far you will travel along the path. Good luck on your journey.

空手 Karate
Warm-Ups

L et's say you have found a place to work out, and you are ready to begin. To remind students of the seriousness of karate studies, the old masters wisely adopted a simple ancient tradition. The tradition was a bow.

When karate students walk into the dojo, they stop at the door and bow. The bow signals they are leaving all worries and cares outside, and that they are prepared to concentrate only on karate.

It is a good idea to get into the habit of bowing as you enter the room where you will work out. You may feel a bit foolish at first, but you'll soon get used to the move, and it will remind you to clear your mind before starting your training session.

Counting in Japanese

To make your training sessions more authentic, learn to count to ten in Japanese. All the exercises in this book call for ten repetitions, or sets of ten repetitions.

One	Ichi	EE-CHEE
Two	Ni	NEE
Three	San	SAN
Four	Shi	SHE
Five	Go	GO
Six	Roko	RO-KOO
Seven	Shichi	SHE-CHEE
Eight	Hachi	HA-CHEE
Nine	Ku	KOO
Ten	Ju	JOO

Memorize the pronunciation of two numbers a day, and you will know them all very quickly. Repeat the numbers aloud when you perform the warm-ups.

Starting the Training Session

After students enter the workout area and before beginning the class, they perform a formal bow. The students are called to attention, and then they kneel in the *seiza* (SAY-ZA) position with the tops of the feet flat on the floor, the knees apart, the upper body sitting on the heels, and the hands placed palms down on top of the thighs (see drawing on next page).

15

Seiza Position

From the kneeling position, they place their fists on the floor a shoulder width apart in front of their knees and they bow forward, touching the forehead to the floor. Then they return to the upright seiza position.

The formal bow in a karate class shows respect for the **sensei** (SEN-SAY), or "teacher," the other students in the class, and most importantly for yourself. Even though you are working out in your own home, you should perform the formal bow before beginning your warm-ups. This way you will remind yourself of the seriousness of your karate training.

Warm-Up Exercises

Always stretch out before throwing punches and kicks, so wear loose-fitting, comfortable clothes. You really don't need a **gi** (GEE) — a karate uniform — to be a karate student, but if you want to purchase one because it makes you feel more like the real thing, that's fine. Most karate schools sell uniforms to non-members. If you can manage it, it is a great help to practice in front of a full-length mirror, so you can check to see if you are performing a technique correctly. Ask your mom or dad if you can have one for your dojo. Also, we work out in our bare feet, so take off your shoes and socks.

Whatever you do, don't rush through the warm-ups, and never strain or push too far.

Head Roll

Start by loosening up with 50 jumping jacks. Begin with your feet together and hands at your sides. Jump the feet out to the sides while raising the arms in a circular motion until the hands touch above your head. Then jump back to the starting position with the arms returning to your sides.

HEAD ROLLS Stand upright with the feet about a shoulder width apart, and slowly roll your head in a circle. Start by lowering your head in front, then move it in a circle clockwise. Make sure the head roll feels comfortable. Circle three times clockwise and counterclockwise.

ARM ROTATIONS With your hands in fists, and your elbows locked, swing both arms backwards, then over your head, then forward in a large circle. Complete ten of these arm rotations, then do ten more in the opposite direction.

PUSH-UPS Start with regular push-ups. Lie down with your toes curled on the floor and place your hands (palms down) under your shoulders. Next, tense your body and push off the ground until your elbows lock. Be sure to keep your body straight from the shoulders to the heels.

Try starting with five push-ups, and add a few each week until you are completing three sets of ten.

For the karate push-up, make a fist, and perform the push-up on the front two knuckles. Start out on a rug so you don't injure your knuckles. At first, try a few of the "karate push-ups," then switch to the regular push-ups on the palms. After a while you'll find that you can complete all the push-ups on your knuckles.

Karate Push-Up

SIDE STRETCHES With your arms held straight out to the sides at shoulder level, slowly tilt your upper body down to your left. Next, move back to the upright position, then tilt down to your right. Do three tilts on each side.

LOWER BACK STRETCHES With your elbows slightly bent, place your fists in front of your chest. Twist your upper body first to the right and then to the left, stretching the lower back and waist. Complete ten of these twisting stretches on each side.

Lower Back Stretch

UPPER BODY ROTATIONS Place your hands on your hips, bend forward at the waist, and slowly rotate your upper body to the right in a clockwise motion, then rotate backwards, then to the left, and return to the forward position. Complete three revolutions. Then move in the opposite direction for three more complete circles.

19

STANDING LEG STRETCHES Standing upright with your toes pointed forward, spread your legs to either side about two shoulder widths, then bend forward at the hips, keeping your back as straight as possible, and grab your left ankle with your left hand. Place your right hand on your left knee to keep the knee locked. Slowly pull your head towards your left knee, and hold for a count of ten. Repeat the same stretch with the right leg. Complete three stretches for each side, spreading the legs wider between each stretch.

SEATED LEG STRETCHES Sit on the floor with your legs spread apart as far as they will go. Bend forward at the hips while keeping your back straight, and grab your left ankle. Slowly bring your chest to your left knee, and hold for a count of ten. Then grab the right ankle, bend over to the right knee, and hold for another count of ten. Next, grab both ankles and pull your upper body towards the floor. Hold for the ten count.

Seated Leg Stretch

Spread the legs wider, and repeat the stretches above, working your upper body down to your knees on either side, and then to the center. Complete three of these stretches on each side. Next, place your legs straight out in front of you with the knees locked and the toes curled back towards yourself. Reach forward, grab your ankles, slowly pull yourself forward at the hips, and hold for a count of ten.

When you get good at this, your chest should touch your knees. Repeat this stretch three times.

SIT-UPS For the following exercises, breathe in, tighten the stomach muscles, and move slowly for the best results.

• Lie flat on your back with your knees straight up in the air, your feet off the ground, and the ankles crossed. Place your hands behind your head. Tighten your lower stomach muscles, and slowly curl your knees towards your chest. Do this ten times.

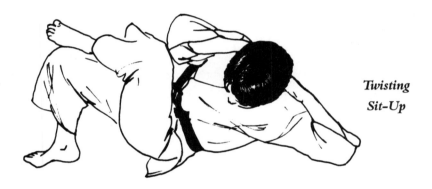

Twisting
Sit-Up

• Bend your right knee and place your right foot on the floor. Place your left ankle on top of your right knee. With your hands behind your head, tighten the stomach muscles, then twist upwards moving your right elbow towards your left knee. Complete ten, then switch the legs and do ten more on the other side.

• With your lower back pushing against the floor, your knees in the air, and your feet on the floor, tighten the stomach muscles, then slowly raise your head and shoulders off the floor. Do ten of these "lift-ups."

The stomach muscles are important in karate, so add a few repetitions each week until you build up to thirty "reps" for each exercise.

Forward Leg Raise

LEG RAISES Stand with your feet on a line about a shoulder width apart and your arms at your sides. Slide your right foot to the rear in a small curve or quarter circle. This step (called a *crescent step*) brings your right foot about six inches further to the outside than when you started. The toes of the rear foot should be "on line" with the heel of the forward foot.

Curl the toes upwards on the right foot and lock the ankle and knee. Swing the right leg forward as high as it will go, keeping the ankle and knee in the "locked" position, then return the leg to the floor to the starting position. While performing the leg raises, try to keep your balance. Complete ten forward leg swings with the right leg, then switch to the left leg and do ten more.

Next, slide the right foot forward in a quarter circle. The heel of the right foot is "on line" with the toes of the rear foot. Again, curl the toes of the right foot and lock the ankle and knee. Swing the right leg backwards and up as far as you can without straining. Complete ten rear leg raises on each side, first with the right leg, then the left.

22

HIP AND KNEE ROTATIONS Place your hands on your hips with your feet a shoulder width apart, and rotate the hips clockwise three times, trying to make each circle larger than the last. Complete the same motion in the opposite direction three times.

For the knee rotations, with your feet close together, bend the knees forward, and place the palms of your hands on top of the knees. Start with your feet flat on the floor. As you rotate the knees in a circle, lift your heels off the floor. When you finish a rotation, return your heels to the floor. Complete three circles clockwise, and then work the knees in the opposite direction.

TOE TOUCHES With your heels together, toes curled upwards, knees locked, and back straight, bend forward slowly at the hips, trying to touch your toes. When you get good at this exercise, you will even be able to place your opened palms on the floor. Complete ten toe touches.

Toe Touch

Finish the warm-ups with 50 more jumping jacks. Now your body is stretched out and you are ready to practice karate!

Lesson 1

Front Punch
• Front Snap Kick
• Tracking the Basics

After finishing the warm-ups, but before learning how to throw the first punch and kick, take a few seconds to relax your body and focus your mind. The best way to relax is by practicing deep breathing.

First, stand with your feet a shoulder width apart. Let your shoulder muscles relax and your arms hang loosely at your sides. Breathe in through your nose and out through your mouth. When you breathe in, your waist should get bigger, and go back to normal when you breathe out. Don't raise your shoulders when you breathe in. Also, when breathing in and out, place the tip of the tongue against the roof of the mouth behind your front teeth, and let the air flow around either side of the tongue.

These deep breathing exercises will help you to relax when you find yourself in a tense situation. After five breaths you will feel the tension leaving your body, and after ten breaths your mind will be focused and you will be better able to face the situation.

The Front Punch
(Upper Body Technique 1)

The Isshinryu front punch is simple to learn because the fist stays vertical (the punch doesn't twist), and it snaps forward on a straight line from the hip to the target. When performed with proper focus and lightning speed, it is a devastating blow.

THE TARGET Imagine an opponent standing directly in front of you. Your target is the center of the body, just above the belt.

THE FIST Hold out both hands, palms up, and slowly curl your fingers into fists. The thumbs are placed over the first two fingers, locking the fists in place (see drawings). Place your fists above your hips with the palms facing inward. Keep your elbows pointed backwards.

Forming the fist

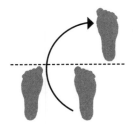

THE STANCE From the *ready stance*, with both feet on line about 12 inches apart, crescent step forward with the right foot into a *seisan* (SAY-SAN) *stance*.

25

THE PUNCH Extend the right fist in a straight line from your hip to the center of the imaginary opponent's midsection. Keep the forearm parallel to the floor, and stop while you still have some bend in your elbow. The hitting surface of the fist is the front two knuckles (see drawing).

Hitting surface

THE SHOUT The moment the fist hits the target, the karateka adds a shout, called a *kiai* (KEE-AYE). The sudden loud shout startles the opponent, and adds power to the technique. The sound of the kiai varies from person to person, but it frequently is an explosive "HAI!"

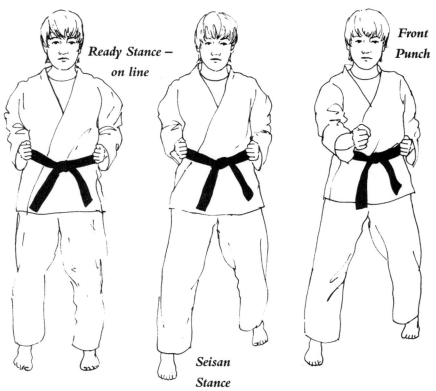

Ready Stance – on line

Front Punch

Seisan Stance

CHECK POSITION With your right arm extended in the punch, place your left fist (palm downwards) between your right elbow and your rib cage on the front right side. This helps you to measure the forward position of the arm after throwing the punch.

RETURN TO START Snap the right fist back to your hip, and at the same time return your right foot to the "on line" position. If you are working in front of a mirror, use your image as a target. Extend the punch, and check to make sure it is centered above the belt.

Power for the front punch comes mostly from the legs and hips. After months of practicing the punch, you will notice how the hips turn and add power while the punch snaps forward and back. Perform the front punch ten times on each side.

The Front Snap Kick
(Lower Body Technique 1)

The front snap kick is a powerful technique because it works the large leg muscles with a snapping action. Like the front punch for the upper body, the front snap kick is the most important lower-body technique to master.

THE TARGET The front snap kick is aimed at the stomach or groin of an opponent in front of you.

THE STANCE With both feet on line and hands on hips (fingers together and pointing forward and thumbs pointing backwards), crescent step with the right foot into a rear seisan stance.

Some lower-body basics call for the hands on the hips; for more advanced kicks, the hands are held in a forward guard position (see pages 37 and 38). The reason for learning kicks with the hands on the hips is to help you balance. As you become more proficient with the lower body, and to add variety to your workout, you can switch to the guard position for all the kicks.

THE CHAMBER Curl up the toes of the right foot, and raise the right leg until the top of your thigh is parallel to the floor. Keep

Rear Seisan Stance   *Chambering
the kick*

the right foot cocked underneath as close to the back of the thigh as possible. This position is called **the chamber**.

THE SNAP Keeping the toes curled and ankle locked, swing the right foot forward. Just before the leg would normally lock at the knee, hit the target with the ball of the foot. Kiai at the moment of impact. Practice snapping the foot forward and then back into the cocked position under the thigh. When done correctly, the kick snaps forward then back at an even faster pace.

RETURN TO START After the snap kick, the foot returns to the chamber. Then place the foot down in the rear seisan stance.

When working on the form of the kick, hold each position for a second or two. After you become familiar with the moves, they should flow together in a fluid, snapping action.

Practice this kick in front of a full-length mirror so you can see exactly what is happening. Pretend your image is the attacker, and snap the kick at the groin or stomach area.

Complete ten snap kicks with each leg.

Front Snap Kick

Tracking the Basics

After learning the form for the front punch and front snap kick, it is time to practice walking the techniques. Instead of practicing techniques you've learned in place, you incorporate them into walking movements forward and backwards. Walking the techniques is called tracking.

You will need enough space to take several steps. A hallway is an ideal spot for walking the front punch and front snap kick.

THE FRONT PUNCH From the ready stance with both fists on your hips, crescent step forward with the right foot into a seisan stance. Plant the right foot **(1)**, then punch with the right arm and kiai. Keep the arm extended.

Crescent step forward with the left foot, plant the foot **(2)**, and as the left punch snaps forward with a kiai, the right punch snaps back to the hip. Walk back and forth several times, throwing a front punch with each crescent step.

THE FRONT SNAP KICK For the front snap kick, start with your right foot in a rear seisan stance. Place your hands on your hips palms down with the thumbs pointing backwards.

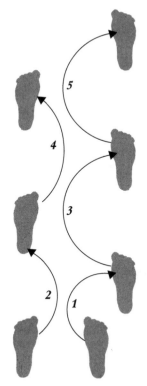

Walking the Front Punch

Front Punch

Front Snap Kick

Perform the front snap kick exactly as you learned it in this chapter. After the snapping action and kiai, instead of returning the kicking foot to the rear, place the foot in a forward seisan stance. Follow with a snap kick with the left foot, then step the foot forward.

Practice walking the front snap kick back and forth. Snap the kicking foot back into the chamber faster than it snaps forward.

Combining the Snap Kick and Front Punch

For variety, try combining the techniques. Start with the right foot in a rear seisan stance and the left fist in a forward position (as if you just finished throwing a left punch). The right fist is on the right hip.

Throw a front snap kick with the right leg and kiai, then place the foot down in a forward seisan stance. Follow with a right front punch and kiai. When the right punch lands, the left fist snaps back to the left hip.

Keep the right arm extended, and now throw the left front snap kick. Place the kicking foot down in a forward seisan stance, then follow with a left front punch. As the left punch lands, the right fist snaps back to the right hip. Kiai with each technique.

Continue tracking the combination front snap kick and punch, moving back and forth several times.

Lesson 2

Reverse Punch •Side Snap Kick • Fighting Stance and Reverse Punch

Believe it or not, the eyes are an important part of karate training. First, they help to keep your mind focused. Karatekas do not look all around the room, and they do not become distracted. Second, the look in your eyes can tell an opponent you mean business. So you need to practice the fierce karate look called "tiger eyes."

Standing with your palms against the sides of your legs, look directly at your eyes in a mirror. Next, tilt your chin down about a half an inch, so you are looking from under your eyebrows. Keep your eyes focused straight ahead.

This is what is called "tiger eyes." The old karate masters were known to terrify their opponents with the fierce look of their eyes. Keep practicing the "tiger eyes" during your training sessions.

The Reverse Punch
(Upper Body Technique 2)

The reverse punch is a quick, natural technique thrown with the arm opposite the forward foot.

THE TARGET The reverse punch is aimed at the midsection of an imaginary opponent in front of you.

THE STANCE From the ready stance, with your knees slightly bent, and your fists on your sides above the hips, crescent step forward with the left foot into a seisan stance.

THE PUNCH Extend the right fist on a straight line toward the target. Kiai. Hold the fist extended, and check for a slight bend in the elbow. Keep the fist tightly curled, and center the punch above the belt area. Your forearm should be parallel to the floor.

RETURN TO START As the right fist snaps back to the hip, the left foot returns to the starting position. Both moves happen at the same time, so the fist returns to the hip the instant the foot lands.

Reverse Punch

34

On the other side: crescent step forward with the right foot into a seisan stance, punch with the left fist, kiai, and return to the starting position. Perform ten reverse punches on each side.

As you repeat the moves, add more snap to the punches.

The Side Snap Kick
(Lower Body Technique 2)

The rapid-fire, side snap kick involves body shifting and is very effective when facing two attackers (with one standing to your side). The kick starts the same as the front snap kick, with hands on hips and the right foot in a rear seisan stance.

THE CAT STANCE
Turn the left foot and hips 45 degrees to the right, point the right foot directly to the side, lower the hips, bend the knees, and shift all the body weight to the left leg. Lift the right heel off the floor (the ball of the foot remains on the floor). This is called a *cat stance.*

Cat Stance

35

Chambering the kick

THE TARGET The target for the side snap kick is the groin or stomach of an opponent standing to your side.

THE CHAMBER Lift the right leg with the toes curled, the ankle locked, and the heel tucked beneath the thigh until the top of the leg from the knee to the hip is parallel to the floor. Now with the leg cocked in the chamber, the kick is ready to snap into action.

THE SNAP The kicking action is the same as the front snap kick, but, with the hips pivoted, the kick is delivered at a 90-degree angle to the side. Snap out the lower leg with the toes curled, hitting the imaginary attacker with the ball of the foot. Kiai.

Side Snap Kick

36

RETURN TO START After the side snap kick returns to the chamber, pivot the hips back to the front starting position, and lower the kicking foot to the floor in a rear seisan stance.

When practicing this kick in front of a mirror, turn to the side so the mirror is to your right. Then when you pivot the hip and snap out the kick, you can see if the ball of your foot is striking the midsection of an imaginary attacker.

How many times should you perform a new technique after you've just learned it? Twenty-five times? Fifty? It depends on your karate spirit!

The Fighting Stance and Reverse Punch

To form the fighting stance, start with the right foot to the rear in a seisan stance. Spin on the balls of the feet 45 degrees to the right and move the right foot to the rear about eight inches (see diagram below). Bend the knees slightly and keep the upper body upright.

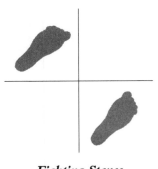

Fighting Stance

Both arms are bent at the elbow in a guard position, with the left fist held out about a foot and a half from the chest. The right fist is about six inches behind the left fist. If you are looking at yourself in a mirror, both fists line up under the chin. (See positioning of hands and feet in drawing on next page.)

For the reverse punch, keep the left arm in place to block, and lower the right fist towards the right hip. The reverse punch snaps across the stomach towards the midsection of the opponent, then back to the hip. Try throwing a reverse punch from the fighting stance on the opposite side (with the left foot to the rear).

Because the reverse punch from this stance is partially hidden by the forward blocking arm, it adds the element of surprise to the technique.

Fighting Stance

Lesson 3

Uppercut
• Knee Kick
• Slip Step and Reverse Punch

The karate student trains by repeating upper- and lower-body techniques over and over. Even black belts with years of experience spend lots of time practicing the "basics."

Why this repetition? Because when you travel the path of the martial arts, you are trying to be the best you can be, and that takes time and effort. Each technique must be practiced over and over, until the form and speed and power and timing all come together to create a lightning-fast punch or kick.

Another reason for repeating the basic techniques is because, when a dangerous situation arises, you want to react quickly with focus and control. The repetitions train your body to react instantly.

During each training session, after completing the warm-ups, perform all the techniques learned in the previous lessons at least ten times, concentrating on form, then adding speed and snap.

The Uppercut
(Upper Body Technique 3)

When less than an arm's length away from an opponent, you won't have as many punching and kicking options because there is little room to maneuver. But you can learn several powerful karate techniques that are very effective in close quarters.

THE TARGET The uppercut, one of those excellent "in-fighting" techniques, is delivered to the chin of an imaginary opponent.

THE STANCE From the ready stance with your feet "on line," place your fists on your hips. Crescent step forward with the right foot into a seisan stance.

Uppercut

UPPERCUT DYNAMICS Imagine a string held taut from your hip bone to the chin of an imaginary opponent. The punch follows directly along that line. As the punch travels upwards from the hip, turn the fist one quarter to the right as shown. When the punch is fully extended, the palm of your fist is facing you.

40

FOCUS UPPERCUT Check these four points to make sure the punch is properly focused: 1) the uppercut forms a 90-degree angle at the elbow; 2) the wrist is straight (a bent wrist may be injured); 3) hit the chin with the first two knuckles of the fist; 4) kiai.

The uppercut drives the opponent's chin up and back.

RETRACT PUNCH After completing the uppercut, the fist snaps back to the hip, and at the same time the right foot returns to the starting position.

Practice throwing the uppercut from both sides. Then for variety try throwing the punch from the reverse position. For the "reverse uppercut," instead of a crescent step with your right foot, start with the left, then snap the right uppercut to the chin.

Perform the uppercut ten times on each side, then switch to the reverse uppercut and throw that punch ten times.

The Knee Kick
(Lower Body Technique 3)

The knee kick is very damaging and should be used only if an attacker is threatening to hurt you. This is not a technique, for example, to be used in sparring matches where the object is only to score points.

THE TARGET This kick is aimed at the side of the knee of an opponent standing in front and slightly to the right of you.

THE STANCE With your hands on your hips, crescent step with the right foot into a rear seisan stance.

THE CHAMBER Raise the right knee as high into the chamber as possible. Lock the ankle and curl up the toes.

THE BODY SHIFT With the right knee high in the chamber, on the ball of the left foot turn 45 degrees to the left.

*Chamber, shift
and kick*

THE KICK As the body shifts, thrust the right leg out, locking the knee and hip, to strike the side of the opponent's knee with the blade side (outside edge) of the foot (see drawing). Kiai.

RETURN TO START As the knee returns high into the chamber, turn on the ball of the left foot so you are facing forward again. Then place the right foot down in a rear seisan stance.

Complete ten repetitions of the knee kick with each foot.

Tracking the Slip Step and Reverse Punch

The slip step allows you to move quickly in and out of range of your target while developing forward momentum for your punches.

Take the fighting stance, with your right foot to the rear. Are your hips and feet on a 45-degree angle? Are your fists lined up under your chin? Is your left fist forward?

Learning the slip step is easy. Slide the left foot forward about twelve inches (1). Next, the right foot slides forward (2) so that you end up with both feet about twelve inches in front of where you started.

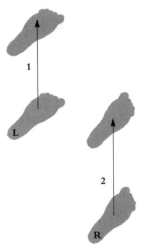

Slip Step

43

Try several slip steps forward, then slip step in the reverse direction (the rear foot moves back, followed by the forward foot). Watch the movement of your head in the mirror as you do the step. Rather than bobbing up and down, your head should stay on a straight line as you slip step backwards and forward.

To add the reverse punch, lower your right fist to the hip. Slide the left foot forward, then begin the punch. As the left foot is planted, the punch is fully extended. Kiai. Then slip step forward with the rear foot and retract the fist to the hip. The forward momentum of the slip step causes the punch to explode outward.

Practice the slip step and reverse punch backwards and forward, first on the right side, then on the left. As you become more comfortable with the slip step, add speed and cover more distance when moving forward and backwards.

Lesson 4
Low Block and Reverse Punch •Heel Push Kick •Crossover Step and Reverse Punch

"Never strike first," warned the old karate masters. "Seek peace instead." That might sound strange when you are learning punches and kicks. But the masters were very wise. They knew that it took long hours of training and lots of confidence and courage to be able to say, "I don't want to fight."

The "never strike first" idea is so important that the masters made it a part of the katas, so their students would never forget it. After the opening bow, the Isshinryu karateka places both hands in front of the chest. The left hand is open and the right hand, placed in the left palm, is a closed fist. The open palm is a reminder to seek peace first, and the closed fist is a sign which says "I will fight only as a last resort."

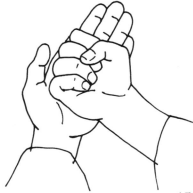

This "never strike first" rule of karate is similar to the idea popular on the streets and playgrounds today: the one that says you can agree with another person to withdraw from a dangerous situation without losing face. Its sign is the open palm placed over a closed fist.

Low Block – front view

"Never strike first," "squash it," "choose to defuse" — whatever it is called, such ideas teach self-control and offer a peaceful way to avoid fighting.

The Low Block and Reverse Punch
(Upper Body Technique 4)

The "never strike first" idea is built into the moves of the advanced upper body basics. The experienced karateka always reacts to an attack by blocking first. If the block is strong enough, it can stop a fight before it starts. The low block and reverse punch combination is the first advanced technique you will learn.

THE TARGET As an attacker throws a low punch or kick, you block, then counterpunch to the midsection.

STACK THE FISTS From the ready stance with both fists on the hips, move the left fist across the body, placing it on top of the right fist. This is called "stacking the fists."

Low Block – side view

THE STANCE Crescent step with the right foot into a rear seisan stance.

THE LOW BLOCK Imagine an attacker before you, throwing a low punch or kick. With the fingers tightly curled in a fist and the forearm muscles tensed, sweep the left arm down and across the front of the body in a blocking motion. Exhale sharply.

The low block moves in a quarter circle, ending with a slight bend in the elbow, and the fist about twelve inches out in front of the left leg. Keep the palm of the left fist facing to the right. You are blocking the imaginary attack with the muscles of the forearm.

THE REVERSE PUNCH After the block, the right fist snaps forward to the midsection of the opponent in front of you. Kiai. As the right punch extends, the left fist retracts from the low block, returning to your hip (the punch hits the target and the left fist lands back at the hip at the same time).

RETURN TO START Snap the right fist back to the hip, while returning the right foot forward to the ready stance.

Practice the low block and reverse punch, first on the right side, and then on the left. For the left side, stack the fists (right on top of left) on the left hip. Crescent step back with the left foot into a rear seisan stance, and block low with the right arm.

As you become familiar with the block–punch sequence, work on timing. The rear crescent step and the low block are done at the same time. Follow through with the reverse punch as the opposite arm retracts to the hip. In a regular workout, complete the combination ten times on each side.

The Heel Push Kick
(Lower Body Technique 4)

The heel push kick serves two special functions: first, it is a "pushing" kick that sends an opponent backwards; second, the fully extended leg creates space so the attacker can't reach you with a punch. The heel push kick is the "knock down the door" technique that you see so often in the movies.

THE TARGET An opponent facing you is too close. You aim for the midsection.

THE STANCE Crescent step with the right foot into a rear seisan stance.

THE CHAMBER Raise the right knee towards your chest as tight as you can, and hold. Keep the ankle locked and the foot tucked under the thigh. Curl the toes upwards.

THE KICK Extend the leg straight out from the hip, locking the knee with the foot raised waist high. As the knee locks out, thrust

Heel Push Kick

49

the hips forward and kiai for extra power. Curl back the toes so the heel becomes the kicking surface. Check in a mirror (sideview) to make sure your hips are forward and your heel extends beyond the ball of the foot.

RETRACT THE KICK Return the knee to the chamber position, then place the right foot down in a rear seisan stance.

Complete ten repetitions of the heel push kick with each leg.

Tracking the Crossover Step and Reverse Punch

Both the slip step and the crossover step move the karateka backwards and forward, but the crossover step covers almost twice the distance in the same amount of time.

The slip step you have learned is effective when fighting in close. The crossover step works well when you are out of range of the opponent's attack and want to move in quickly to throw a technique.

For the crossover step, start with the basic fighting stance, right foot to rear, knees bent, and both feet on a 45-degree angle. Now bring the right foot back six inches, making the stance wider.

Lift the right foot off the floor in a crossover step on a straight line forward, placing it down in front of the left foot. Keep the knees bent. Follow with the left foot, placing it down in front of the right foot. Look at your feet. They should be in a wide fighting stance.

Move backwards and forward using the crossover step. To move backwards, reverse the action of the feet by moving the left foot back and then the right foot. Avoid bobbing up and down when performing the crossover step. Glide back and forth on a straight line with your knees bent and your upper body at the same level.

From the crossover step, you can attack by throwing the reverse punch two ways. For the first, the right reverse punch snaps forward a second before you start the crossover step with the right foot.

Wide Fighting
Stance

Crossover Step

51

Kiai. The forward momentum of the snapping punch pulls the body into the crossover step. Finish the right crossover step, and move the left foot to the forward position.

For the second way to attack, crossover step with the right foot and snap out the right reverse punch at the same time. The punch hits the target as the right foot lands. Kiai. Follow through by stepping forward with the left foot. Avoid hesitation in the crossover step by keeping your forward momentum as fluid as possible.

Start with the right foot to the rear, and practice the crossover step with both reverse punches. Then switch, and practice the crossover step and reverse punch starting with the left foot to the rear.

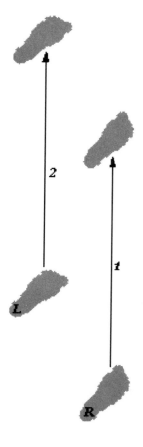

Crossover Step

Lesson 5

Mid Block and Reverse Punch • Knee Punch • Backfist

K arate training teaches you to focus your mind. This is the key to becoming a champion. The old karate masters demanded the highest level of concentration from their students because they knew that fully aware karatekas learn more quickly and carry those focusing skills into their everyday lives. "Concentrate so hard that your hair feels as if it is on fire," the old masters told their students.

You can develop awesome powers of concentration by following these simple directions:

• Remember to stop and bow when entering and leaving the room where you work out. This serves to focus your attention on what you are doing.

• Practice the "tiger eyes" to place yourself in a "zone." This helps you to zero in on your target, while at the same time it keeps you aware of your surroundings.

• Use the power of your mind to create imaginary attackers surrounding you. Every technique is thrown at them.

During your workouts, strive to be of "one mind." Center all your attention on perfecting the karate techniques. When you are at school, walking down the street, or playing, practice being aware of what is happening around you. Imagine that you are able to look in all directions at once.

Practicing awareness helps develop an early alarm system. When something dangerous is about to happen, the sooner you are aware of that situation, the better you will be able to avoid it.

The Mid Block and Reverse Punch
(Upper Body Technique 5)

The mid block and reverse punch is the second of the advanced block–punch combinations.

THE TARGET As an attacker throws a punch to your chest, you block and counter with a reverse punch to the midsection.

STACK THE FISTS In the ready stance, stack both fists (left over right) on the right hip.

THE STANCE Crescent step with the right foot into a rear seisan stance.

THE MID BLOCK Imagine an attacker throwing a punch to your chest. Sweep the left forearm — with the muscles tensed — in a

Mid Block —
front and side view

quarter-circle blocking action across the stomach and chest, stopping the fist in front of the left shoulder. Exhale sharply.

At the end of the block, the fist is shoulder high, and the elbow is bent at a 90-degree angle. Because you block with the fore-arm muscles, the palm of the left fist will face to the right at the end of the blocking action.

THE REVERSE PUNCH The right punch snaps forward to the midsection of the attacker. As the right arm punches, the left fist returns from the blocking position to the left hip. The punch hits the target at the same instant the left fist returns to the hip. Kiai, as the punch lands.

RETURN TO START Snap the right fist back to the right hip, while returning the right foot forward to the ready stance.

Work on the timing of this "one-two" combination until the action feels comfortable. The count of "one" is for the block, the count of "two" is for the punch. In your regular workout, complete the moves ten times on each side.

The Knee Punch
(Lower Body Technique 5)

The knee punch is an excellent "in-fighting" technique, used when an opponent is close to you.

THE TARGET The close-in target is the opponent's groin area.

THE STANCE Crescent step with the right foot into a rear seisan stance. Imagine an opponent standing right before you. Place your open palms on his shoulders.

THE LEG CHAMBER Swing the bottom part of the right leg backwards and point the toes to the rear as if performing a dive.

THE KICK Close the hands into fists (imagine grabbing the opponent's shoulders). Pull the closed fists to your hips on either side (you are pulling the upper body of the opponent forward).

Knee Punch –
up and forward

As your fists move towards your hips, drive the knee upwards and forward into the groin. For extra power, the hips pivot forward as the knee drives towards the target. Kiai. Keep the toes pointed downwards.

RETURN TO START Bring the leg back to the starting position with your right foot to the rear. At the same time, move the fists from the hips to the starting shoulder-high position with the hands open and palms facing forward, ready for the next repetition.

Complete ten repetitions of the knee punch with each leg.

Tracking the Backfist

The backfist is quick, it can be used to set up an attack, and when combined with the forward slip step it covers a lot of territory.

Start in the basic fighting stance, left foot to the rear, fists in the guard position, knees bent slightly, and both feet on a 45-degree angle.

Snap the right fist forward leaving a slight bend in the elbow. Use the elbow as a pivot. Hit with the front two knuckles on the bridge of the nose of an imaginary opponent. Kiai. Then snap the fist back to the starting position.

Without moving the feet, practice whipping the fist out to an imaginary target and back. Switch your fighting stance (right foot to the rear), and practice the same whipping action with the left fist.

Backfist

Now let's add the slip step. As you slip step forward with the left foot, add the backfist. When the left foot lands, the backfist whips forward. Kiai. When the right foot slip steps forward, the fist snaps back to the starting position.

Practice tracking the slip step and backfist on both sides. Move as far forward as you can in your workout space, then turn around and practice the moves in the opposite direction.

Lesson 6

空手

High Block and Reverse Punch
•Roundhouse Kick •Backfist and Reverse Punch

*J*n the old days, when a youth approached a karate master and asked to be accepted as a student, often the master would laugh and tell the young person to go away. That sounds cruel, but it takes many years of hard practice to become a karate expert, and the master could not waste time teaching someone who would later disappoint him.

But if the youngster persisted, and was lucky, sometimes the master gave the youth menial tasks to perform, such as sweeping out the dojo. During such times, which often lasted six months or more, the master seemed to pay little attention to the youngster. But it was all a test.

The master wanted to find out if the young person was respectful or a braggart, and if he or she was willing work quietly and efficiently, instead of being lazy and complaining. The master was testing the youngster's attitude.

Even today, "attitude" is most important in a karateka. Attitude defines the kind of person you are. Do you respect yourself and others? Are you ready to train hard? Are you jealous or afraid of those who have better technique than you? Do you make fun of those who have less skill than you do? What kind of answers do you think the master would be looking for to these questions?

The High Block and Reverse Punch
(Upper Body Technique 6)

You have already practiced the low and mid blocks. Next comes the high block.

THE TARGET As an attacker throws a punch to your head, you block and counter with a reverse punch to the midsection.

STACK THE FISTS In the ready stance, stack the fists (left over right), on the right hip.

THE STANCE Crescent step with the right foot into a rear seisan stance.

THE HIGH BLOCK Quickly raise the left forearm, stopping with the fist above eye level. The forearm from the elbow to the wrist forms a 45-degree angle. Bend the wrist slightly (you should be able to see under your left wrist). Exhale sharply.

In the blocking action, the fist makes a quarter turn (moving the thumb side up), exposing the tensed forearm muscles as the blocking surface. (See drawings on opposite page.)

60

High Block —
front and side view

THE REVERSE PUNCH After the left arm blocks the punch to
the head, the right fist snaps forward to the midsection of the
opponent. Kiai. As the right arm punches, the fist of the blocking
arm snaps back to the hip.

RETURN TO START The right fist snaps back to the hip as the right
foot moves forward to the ready stance. The foot lands at the same
time as the fist retracts to the hip.

Practice the high block and reverse punch on both sides. Complete
ten high block and reverse punch combinations on each side.

61

Next, practice the blocks in a sequence without the reverse punches. Start with a left high block, followed by a right mid block, then a left low block, then a right low block, then a left mid block, followed by a right high block.

Stand in front of a mirror and check the blocking action. The low block stops at the side of the thigh; the mid block, fist shoulder high, ends at the side of the shoulder; the high block stops with the wrist just above eye level. Tense the forearm muscles and exhale sharply for each block.

Complete this blocking sequence ten times during your regular workout. To add variety, follow the same sequence but add the reverse punch after each block.

The Roundhouse Kick
(Lower Body Technique 6)

The roundhouse kick flows in a semicircular pattern and uses a hip turn and a snapping leg action to add speed and power to the technique.

THE TARGET The roundhouse kick circles and drives inward toward the midsection of an opponent standing sideways in front of you.

THE STANCE Place your feet together, heel to heel, left foot pointing forward, right foot pointing to the side, forming a 90-degree angle. Move the right foot back about a shoulder width and a half, keeping the heels "on line." Lower the body about six inches by bending the knees. Roughly 70 percent of your body

Chambering the kick

Pivot for the Roundhouse Kick

weight is on the rear leg. This is called a **hominy** (HAH-MINEE) **stance**. Hold the fists in the guard position, left fist forward.

THE LEG CHAMBER

From the hominy stance, move forward, placing your weight on the left leg, and raise the right knee to the side. Keep the kicking leg parallel to the floor, forming a right angle with the left leg, and tuck the heel in close to the back of the thigh. Curl the toes. The kick is now chambered, and the right fist is in a guard position to the side.

THE HIP TURN With the right leg in the chambered position, pivot counterclockwise a quarter turn on the ball of the left foot. The knee of the right leg now points forward. To keep the kicking leg parallel to the floor, imagine pivoting the leg over a tabletop. The right fist moves into the forward guard position.

THE KICK At the end of the quarter turn, using the momentum of the pivoting hip, snap the right foot out striking the midsection of the imaginary opponent with the ball of the foot. Kiai.

Roundhouse Kick

RETRACT THE KICK After delivering the kick, the lower part of the leg snaps back into the chamber. Keep the leg parallel to the floor when retracting the kick. Then lower the kicking leg to the floor to form the *horse stance*.

In the horse stance, both feet are pointed forward and positioned about a shoulder width and a half apart. The knees push out to the sides as if you are riding a horse. The right fist remains in the guard position.

From the beginning when you are standing in the hominy stance, to where you place your feet down in the horse stance, your body turns 180 degrees.

Horse Stance
with fist
in guard position

RETURN TO START From the horse stance, pivot clockwise on the ball of the left foot until you are back in the starting hominy stance.

Complete ten repetitions of the roundhouse kick with each leg.

Tracking the Backfist and Reverse Punch

The backfist and reverse punch combination is an advanced tracking exercise. The backfist can be a scoring technique, or a fake that causes the opponent to raise his guard. If the opponent doesn't block, you score with the backfist. If the opponent raises a guard, you throw a reverse punch to the mid-section.

To practice this scoring combination, get in the basic fighting stance, fists in the guard position, right foot to the rear, knees slightly bent, and the feet pointing 45 degrees to the right.

Standing in place, snap the left fist out, aiming at the bridge of the nose of an imaginary opponent. As the left fist retracts, snap the reverse punch out and back. This one-two combination is performed with lightning speed. Switch and practice the same one-two combination on the other side.

Now add the slip step to move in and out of range of the opponent. Start with the right foot to the rear and the fists in a guard position. Slide the left foot forward and snap out the backfist. The left foot and backfist land at the same time. As the right foot slides forward, snap out the reverse punch.

As you slip step back and forth throwing the backfist–reverse punch combination, count "one-two, one-two," to get used to the proper timing. Practice the combination on both sides, backwards and forward.

Lesson 7

Shuto Strike and Karate Chop • Front Thrust Kick • Backfist, Reverse Punch and Roundhouse Kick

An old saying explains how the young karateka should approach the study of the martial arts. The saying is important to remember when you start to lose interest in the basics, have a problem performing a technique correctly, or don't seem to be making any progress in your training.

"Whatever it takes," my sensei used to say to our class whenever he thought we needed encouragement. It is a simple saying, but it carries a lot of meaning. "Whatever it takes" is a mind-set, part of the mental training of becoming a true martial artist. It means that when the going gets tough, the karateka works longer and harder to succeed.

It is easy to give up and say, "This is too hard," "I can't do this," or, "I don't have time to practice today." The world is full of quitters and complainers. But guess what? They never get anywhere in life.

So when you wonder about spending time training when you could be watching TV, a movie, or playing with your friends, remember: you are being tested to see if you have what it takes to be a champion.

Repeat the saying "Whatever it takes" to yourself, and keep training. You'll be a better karateka because of it. You'll even be a better person.

The Shuto Strike and Karate Chop
(Upper Body Technique 7)

The *shuto* (SHOO-TOE) strike followed by the karate chop involve body shifting, movement of both arms at the same time, and strikes with both hands. The best way to learn this combination is to break it down into parts. When you understand all the moves, put them together in one flowing motion.

THE TARGET The shuto strike snaps forward into the opponent's solar plexus, or pit of the stomach. The karate chop is aimed at the base of the neck and the collarbone.

THE STANCE Place both feet "on line" in a ready stance and the hands on the hips in the opened position (wrist and fingers straight, and thumbs placed on top).

CHAMBER THE SHUTO STRIKE Raise the left hand, palm upwards, and rest the shuto part of the hand (the muscle on the side of the hand opposite the thumb) on the chest. Crescent step with the left foot into a forward seisan stance.

68

*Ready Stance for Shuto
and Chop combination*

*Chambering the
Shuto Strike – palm up*

THE STRIKE Practice this next move slowly at first. In a circular motion, the left hand moves out from the chest about six inches, turns over so the thumb is now facing your chest, then snaps straight forward towards the solar plexus of the imaginary opponent. Exhale sharply.

69

Shuto Strike –
palm down

Arm position for
Karate Chop

The striking surface is the muscle on the side of the left hand, not the fingers. To perform this move correctly, you must move the left elbow forward as you snap out the shuto strike or the fingers become the striking surface. As you become familiar with this move, the crescent step and shuto strike land at the same time. The forward momentum of the step builds power for the strike.

THE KARATE CHOP Raise the right hand to the side, so the arm from the shoulder to the elbow is parallel to the floor. The upper part of the arm (elbow to hand) is held straight up in the air, forming a 90-degree angle at the elbow. The palm faces forward.

To perform the famous "karate chop," the upper torso rotates slightly counterclockwise as the right elbow and shoulder move forward. During the downward motion of the right hand, the palm turns and faces to the left. The karate chop is delivered between the shoulder and neck of the opponent. Picture your hand following a line through the collarbone. Kiai.

Karate Chop

As the right arm strikes down with the karate chop, the left arm returns to the hip.

RETURN TO START Snap the right hand back to the right hip, and return the left foot to the ready stance. Both hands remain in the open position, and the left foot lands the same instant as the right hand reaches the hip. Practice the strikes on both sides following the steps outlined above. Complete the moves in a count of "one – two – three." During a regular workout, perform the shuto strike and karate chop combination ten times on each side.

The Front Thrust Kick
(Lower Body Technique 7)

The front thrust kick combines the forward momentum of a thrusting action with a quick hip turn. Add the power of the leg muscles, and the locking action of the hip and knee, and the result is an explosive lower-body technique.

THE TARGET The front thrust kick is aimed at the midsection of an opponent.

THE STANCE Crescent step with the right foot into the rear seisan stance. Place the fists in a guard position, the left arm held forward.

CHAMBER THE LEG Raise the right knee towards your chest as high as possible. Lock the ankle, curl the toes upwards, and keep the foot tucked under the thigh. Both fists are in the guard position.

Seisan Stance

*Chambering
the kick*

*Hip turn with
kicking leg on
45-degree angle*

THE KICK Keep your eyes on the target. As you spin counter-clockwise over a quarter of a turn on the ball of the left foot, rotate the knee to position the kicking leg to a 45-degree angle, and execute a full hip turn. Thrust out the right leg, locking the hip and knee as shown on page 74. Kiai.

During the kick, the left fist stays close to the chest, while the right arm extends over the kicking leg. When performed correctly, there is a straight line from the right shoulder, through the right hip, to the top of the right heel.

Thrust Kick

When the leg locks out, the position of the kicking foot is important. The heel (the kicking surface) is extended, and the toes are turned slightly towards the floor.

RETRACT THE KICK The knee snaps back into the chamber, remaining parallel to the floor. The right fist retracts to the guard position. Then, lower the kicking leg to the floor in a horse stance. Both fists return to the basic upper–body guard position. The eyes remain on the target.

RETURN TO START From the horse stance, pivot clockwise 90 degrees on the ball of the left foot, returning the right foot to the rear seisan stance.

Complete ten repetitions of the front thrust kick with each leg.

Horse Stance

Tracking the Backfist, Reverse Punch and Roundhouse Kick

The last chapter explained how to combine the backfist and the reverse punch in a scoring combination. The backfist causes the opponent to block high, setting up the reverse punch to the midsection. Now we add a roundhouse kick, which comes from an entirely different direction, making it an effective "finishing" technique. The fight is over after a "finishing" technique is thrown.

Start in a fighting stance with the fists in the guard position. Slip step forward with the left foot and snap the left backfist towards an imaginary opponent's nose. The backfist and left foot land at the same time.

Follow with a front crossover step, right foot over left (see page 50 to review the crossover step). Keep a bend in both knees for the crossover step. The reverse punch snaps forward as the right foot lands.

Raise the left leg, turn the hips clockwise, and snap the leg in a roundhouse kick into the midsection of the opponent. Kiai. Return the left leg to the chamber, then place the left foot down into the fighting stance.

Practice the backfist, reverse punch, roundhouse kick sequence first with the right foot to the rear, then switch to the left foot to the rear. Once you become comfortable with the moves, work on speed so that the techniques flow in rapid-fire succession. Eventually, the timing becomes a quick "one – two – three" count.

Lesson 8

Kata

The old masters knew that their students needed help in remembering all the blocks, punches, and kicks. Also, the students wanted to learn how to apply the techniques in fighting situations. So the masters devised the **kata** (KAH-TAH), a series of moves responding to attacks by imaginary opponents.

Each karate style has several katas showing how blocks, punches, and kicks are used in different circumstances. Sometimes the masters created new katas, and other times they borrowed moves from existing katas.

Katas can be read like chapters in a book, with each chapter covering a different situation. One kata, for example, takes place at night under a full moon. Another occurs on a narrow bridge or in an alleyway, with little room to maneuver around. In still another, the karateka's back is against a wall, allowing only side-to-side movements.

Because there is so much to learn, a kata is taught in stages. During the first stage, the karateka memorizes the correct sequence of the blocks, punches, and kicks. This stage is like a sculptor chipping away at a block of marble, creating a rough form.

Next, when the student knows all the moves, work begins on making the kata more realistic by developing timing and reactions relating to the attacks of the imaginary opponents. This stage is similar to an artist creating the individual features of the sculpture so they are more recognizable.

In the last stage, the kata comes to life as a dramatic story. The kareteka, after mastering all the moves and their meanings, appears to flow through the kata effortlessly, reacting to the imaginary attackers with punches and kicks of blinding speed and accuracy. This last stage is like an artist adding the finishing touches to the sculpture, then polishing its surface, and making it lifelike.

Taikyokyu One

Each kata has a number of sets (series of moves) that follow a basic pattern. For example, *Taikyokyu* (TIE-KYO-KOO) *One*, a basic upper-body kata, consists of blocks and punches, and the sets form an "I-shaped" pattern. The kareteka starts at the top of the "I," facing towards the bottom.

Take your time with this kata. Learning one new set each week is a reasonable goal. Then you can begin work on polishing the kata, which takes — are you ready for this? — years! The experts practice all their katas daily, trying to improve the form, power, and speed of the techniques.

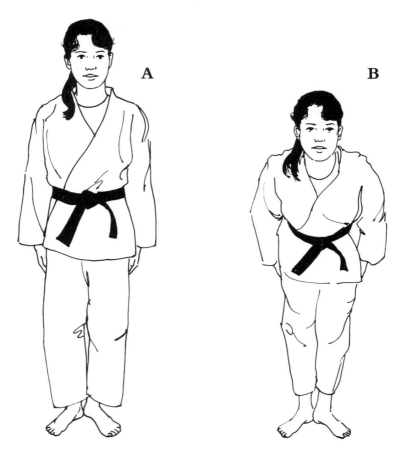

THE OPENING Stand with your hands open, palms pressing against your sides, heels together, and toes pointed at a 30-degree angle **(A)**.

Crescent step forward and to the left with the left foot. This move signals that the kata is about to begin, and it also serves to "test the ground" in front of the karateka. Then return the left foot to the starting position. With your hands still at your sides, bow about twelve inches forward, bending at the hips **(B)** but keeping the back straight. Imagine that an attacker is standing in front of you. As you bow, keep your eyes on the person's chest.

78

Return your upper body to the upright position, then raise your left hand to the chest in an open position, palm facing inward. Immediately, raise the right hand in a fist, placing it behind the open left hand (C). The open hand signifies "peace" (the "never strike first" karate philosophy). The closed fist signals the karateka's resolve to fight when life is in danger or when there is no other alternative.

Next, move the right foot about twelve inches out to the side, then close both hands into fists and place them about twelve inches in front of the hips with the elbows slightly bent (D).

1a   1b   1c

SET 1 Move the left foot next to the right, stack your fists (left over right) on the right hip, and turn on the ball of the right foot 90 degrees to the left. Place the left foot down in a forward seisan stance **(1a)**.

Next, move the left arm in front of your face with the fist over your head, then to the left side of your body. The arm forms a 90-degree angle with the elbow on line with the left shoulder, and the forearm and fist are held upright. Next, the left forearm sweeps to the front in a cross block in response to a right chest-high punch thrown by an imaginary attacker **(1b)**. To counter, step forward with the right foot into a seisan stance, and throw a right mid-body punch **(1c)**. Kiai.

2a   2b   2c

SET 2 Stack the fists (right over left) on the left hip. Lift the right foot off the floor and spin clockwise 180 degrees on the ball of the left foot. Replace the right foot in a forward seisan stance. Now you are facing in the opposite direction **(2a)**. Cross block with the right arm and exhale sharply **(2b)**. The right cross block is in response to a left chest-high punch thrown by an imaginary attacker.

Step forward with the left foot into a seisan stance and throw a mid-body punch with the left fist **(2c)**. Kiai. (The first two sets move in opposite directions across the top of the "I.")

3a

SET 3 Stack the fists (left over right) on the right hip, lift the left foot slightly off the ground and spin 90 degrees to the left on the ball of the right foot. Now you should be facing in the same direction as when you started the kata.

Place the left foot down in a forward seisan stance; perform a low block with the left arm, exhaling sharply **(3a)**. The blocking arm stops with the fist about twelve inches in front of the left leg. The tensed muscles of the forearm are used as the blocking surface.

The left low block is in response to a kick or a right low punch by an attacker standing in front of you.

Take three steps forward, each time into a seisan stance. With the first right step, throw a right mid–body punch **(3b)**; then with the left, throw a left mid–body punch **(3c)**, followed by another right step and a last right mid–body punch **(3d)**. Kiai with each punch. After the low block you are pushing the opponent back with a series of punches.

3b

3c

3d

SET 4 With the right foot in a forward seisan stance, stack the left fist over the right on the right hip. Then spin counterclockwise on the ball of the right foot 270 degrees, into a left foot forward seisan stance.

Raise the left fist into a high block position and exhale sharply **(4a)**. The left high block is in response to an attacker throwing a right-hand punch to the face. Then step forward with the right foot into a seisan stance, and throw a mid-body punch with the right fist **(4b)**. Kiai.

4a

4b

SET 5 Stack the fists (right over left) on the left hip, then spin on the ball of the left foot 180 degrees, and place the right foot down in a forward seisan stance.

Throw a right high block (in response to an attacker throwing a lef-hand punch to the face), exhale sharply, then step forward with the left foot into a seisan stance, and throw a mid-body punch with the left fist **(5a, b)**. Kiai. (Sets 4 and 5 move in opposite directions across the bottom of the "I.")

5a

5b

SET 6 Stack the fists (left over right) on the right hip. Lift the left foot slightly off the ground, and spin on the ball of the right foot one quarter turn to the left. You should be facing up the center of the "I."

Place the left foot down in a forward seisan stance, and at the same time perform a low block with the left arm **(6a)**. Exhale sharply.

6a

The left low block is in response to a kick or a right low punch by an attacker.

Take three steps forward, each time into a seisan stance (see opposite page), first with the right and throw a right mid–body punch **(6b)**, then with the left and throw a left mid–body punch **(6c)**, followed by another right and a last right mid–body punch **(6d)**. Kiai with each punch.

After the low block, you are pushing the opponent back with a series of punches.

6d

6c

6b

SET 7 With the right foot in a forward seisan stance, stack the fists (left over right) on the right hip. Then spin counterclockwise 270 degrees on the ball of the right foot. Place the left foot down in a forward seisan stance.

Sweep the left fist across the stomach and chest in a mid–body block and exhale sharply **(7a)**. The left mid–body block is in response to a chest-high right punch from an attacker. Step forward with the right foot into a seisan stance, and throw a mid–body punch with the right fist **(7b)**. Kiai.

SET 8 Stack the fists (right over left) on the left hip. Lift the right foot off the floor and spin clockwise 180 degrees on the ball of the left foot so you are facing in the opposite direction. Place the right foot down in a forward seisan stance.

Throw a mid–body block with the right arm, and exhale sharply **(8a)**. The right mid–body block is in response to a chest–high left punch from an attacker. Step with the left foot into a forward seisan stance, and throw a left–hand mid–body punch **(8b)**. Kiai. (Sets 7 and 8 move in opposite directions across the top of the "I.")

A

B

THE ENDING On the ball of the right foot, spin counterclockwise 90 degrees. Place both feet "on line," about twelve inches apart, toes pointed forward. Hold the fists about twelve inches in front of the hips with the elbows slightly bent. You should be facing in the same direction as when you started the kata **(A)**.

Move the right foot next to the left. Raise the left hand chest high, palm open and facing inward, and place the right fist

90

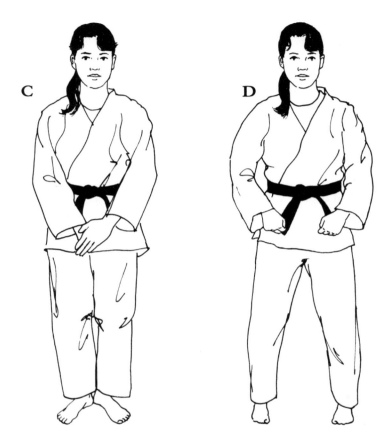

behind the opened palm **(B)**. Keeping the wrists straight, move both hands downwards so the palm of the left hand spins on the top of the right fist. Continue the downward motion of the hands, stopping just below the belt **(C)**.

Finally, the right foot returns twelve inches to the right, and the fists are placed in front of the hips, the elbows slightly bent **(D)**. The kata is finished.

Practicing Kata

The masters believed that practicing kata was the most important part of karate training, even more important than sparring! They knew that kata training prepared students for life. They realized, too, that the most difficult opponents karatekas face are themselves. Often we have too much fear, or we are too cocky, or we think we are going to fail, or we are too lazy.

Katas teach us how to overcome these shortcomings through constant practice. We learn a kata by diligently performing it over and over, for years. The practice makes us grow and develop. In time, the kata becomes a part of ourselves, and our shortcomings slowly disappear.

The lesson the masters want you to learn from kata is that if you want to do something in life and you keep working at it, eventually you will succeed.

Your Karate Future

By working your way carefully through all the lessons in this book, you have gained a valuable foundation for your karate studies. But learning all the techniques is not the same as mastering them.

The study of karate is really a lifelong goal. People spend years trying to perfect the punches and kicks, the tracking exercises, and the katas. They do this to keep healthy and stay in shape; to learn self-defense; to feel more self-confident; and to become more focused human beings in better control of their actions and their lives. They realize they are each on "the path" to becoming a better person.

Now that you have finished this book, you have a decision to make. You could continue your workout sessions, trying to improve your stamina, focus, speed, timing, and power. That's fine, and this book and others that are more advanced that are available to you will serve you well in that endeavor. You might also, however, be interested in joining a nearby school to continue your formal training.

If you decide to consider some formal schooling, you should know what to look for before signing up for classes. Schools vary widely in their approaches and training methods, and you must be certain that you are joining a school that is right for you. Don't be too concerned about the variety of styles taught today, and don't be fooled by people claiming their style is the best. The wise sensei will tell you there are many excellent styles to choose from, and that you should select a style that suits your needs. Ask a parent to go with you to watch a class. Talk to students from the school. Listen to the way the instructor addresses the students. Keep your eyes and ears open.

When visiting a school, look for the answers to these questions: Is there a balanced approach to the study of karate, or are they only interested in sparring? Is the instruction carefully controlled, or are students walking around talking to one another, and doing whatever they please? Do the instructors take the time to explain techniques and concepts, or are they only "doing their job" to make money? What does a promotion cost? What are the qualifications of the instructors? Who is doing the actual teaching? Is respect taught in the dojo? Is the emphasis on learning solid techniques, rather than trying to impress with flashy spinning kicks? Is the major interest winning trophies at tournaments? (Winning trophies is fun, but it should not be a school's major goal.)

If you have the good fortune to locate a sensei you like and respect, if you feel comfortable with the training program, and if you can afford the fees, then you might want to join that school for a trial period and see how it works out. If not, your local library and bookstore are sure to have a number of karate books, written for various levels, that will help you to continue studying the art of karate on your own.

At the close of the introductory chapter I told you about the martial arts path you were beginning to travel. By now, you have taken several steps along the way. I wish you continued success on your personal journey!

Index